920
Dev

Devillier, Christy, 1971-
Lewis & Clark

Lewis & Clark

SOUTHERN HEIGHTS ELEMENTARY

A Buddy Book
by
Christy DeVillier

ABDO
Publishing Company

VISIT US AT

www.abdopub.com

Published by ABDO Publishing Company, 4940 Viking Drive, Edina, Minnesota 55435.
Copyright © 2001 by Abdo Consulting Group, Inc. International copyrights reserved in all
countries. No part of this book may be reproduced in any form without written permission
from the publisher.

Printed in the United States.

Edited by: Michael P. Goecke
Contributing Editor: Matt Ray
Image Research: Deborah Coldiron, Susan Will
Graphic Design: Jane Halbert
Cover Photograph: courtesy of Library of Congress, Washington, D.C.
Interior Photographs/Illustrations: pages 8, 9, 14 & 23: courtesy of Library of Congress,
Washington, D.C.; page 4: courtesy of The Mariners' Museum, Newport News, VA; pages 5,
27, & 28: Deborah Coldiron; pages 15 & 24: North Wind Picture Archives; pages 21 & 25:
Denise Esner; page 22: Maria Hosley

Library of Congress Cataloging-in-Publication Data

Devillier, Christy, 1971-
    Lewis and Clark / Christy Devillier.
        p. cm. — (First biographies)
    Includes index.
    ISBN 1-57765-595-8
    1. Lewis, Meriwether, 1774-1809—Juvenile literature. 2. Clark, William,
    1770-1838—Juvenile literature. 3. Lewis and Clark Expedition (1804-1806)—Juvenile
    literature. 4. Explorers—West (U.S.)—Biography—Juvenile literature. 5. West
    (U.S.)—Discovery and exploration—Juvenile literature. [1. Lewis, Meriwether,
    1774-1809. 2. Clark, William, 1770-1838. 3. Explorers. 4. Lewis and Clark Expedition
    (1804-1806). 5. West (U.S.)—Discovery and exploration.] I. Title.

F592.7 .D48 2001
917.804'2—dc21

                                                                    2001022299

Table of Contents

Why Are They Famous?

Meriwether Lewis and William Clark are famous American explorers. They explored the Western United States. This happened in the early 1800's. This was before the West was settled. Back then, only Native Americans lived in the West. Nobody else knew much about this land.

Lewis and Clark's trip, or expedition, was long and hard. It lasted for two years and four months. Lewis and Clark traveled over 8,000 miles (12,872 km). They learned a lot about the West. The Lewis and Clark Expedition was a grand success!

William Clark

William Clark was born August 1, 1770. He was born in Caroline County, Virginia. He had nine brothers and sisters. One of his brothers was George Rogers. George Rogers Clark was a hero of the American Revolutionary War. George taught William Clark about living in the wild.

William Clark

Clark served in the Kentucky militia. The militia is made up of people who are not soldiers.

Clark was an officer in the regular army by 1792. In 1794, he fought in the battle of Fallen Timbers.

Meriwether Lewis

Meriwether Lewis

Meriwether Lewis was from Virginia, too. He was born on August 18, 1774, near Charlottesville.

Lewis's father fought in the American Revolution. He died when Lewis was only five years old.

In 1794, Lewis joined the militia. In 1801, Lewis was an Army Captain in Pittsburgh. There, he met Lieutenant William Clark. Lewis and Clark became friends.

Lewis worked with President Thomas Jefferson in 1801. Lewis was the President's secretary. This was a very important job.

First Steps

On February 28, 1803, the United States decided to explore the West. President Thomas Jefferson wanted to find out more about this land. Also, he hoped to find a river that ran to the Pacific Ocean. President Jefferson thought this river, or "Northwest Passage," would make the country rich.

Thomas Jefferson

President Jefferson asked Lewis to explore the West. Lewis agreed to lead the expedition. Lewis wanted someone to help him. So, he asked his friend, William Clark. Clark said yes.

Great Friends, Natural Leaders

Lewis and Clark were great friends. They had a lot in common. They were about the same age. They were smart and brave. Both men had spent time on the frontier.

Lewis and Clark were natural leaders. They worked well together. Each man had different strengths.

Lewis scouted land ahead of the expedition.

Lewis was good at noticing little things. He liked to be by himself more than Clark. He was quiet.

Lewis was a good writer, too. He wrote about the animals, flowers, and trees he saw on the expedition.

Clark was good at mapping the land.

William Clark was not quiet like Lewis. Clark was fun-loving. He liked to joke with everyone.

Clark took care of many things on the expedition. He chose where they camped. He oversaw the building of boats and housing. Clark was very good at sailing on the river. He gathered a lot of facts from Native Americans. Clark made good maps, too.

Corps Of Discovery

Lewis and Clark carefully chose about 30 men for the expedition. Some of these men were soldiers and rivermen. President Jefferson called Lewis and Clark's group the "Corps of Discovery."

The Corps of Discovery

Lewis and Clark met many Native Americans.

Lewis brought his dog on the expedition, too. Lewis's dog's name was Seaman.

Together, Lewis and Clark prepared for the trip. They gathered supplies. They took canned food, medicine, presents for Native Americans, tools, and guns.

An Exciting Adventure

Lewis and Clark's expedition began on May 14, 1804. They started near St. Louis, Missouri. They sailed up the Missouri River. Each day, they traveled about 14 miles (23 km). They did not travel in the winter.

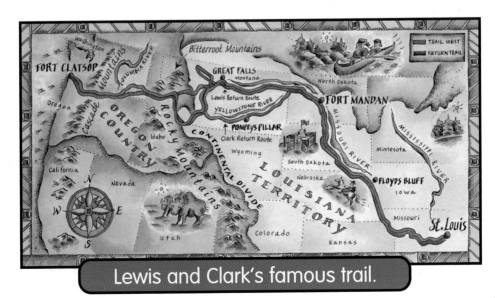

Lewis and Clark's famous trail.

The Corps of Discovery sailed in special boats. One was a keelboat. The keelboat was about 55 feet (17 m) long. It was about eight feet (2.4 m) wide. The other two boats were pirogues. Pirogues are like canoes. They were smaller than the keelboat.

A keelboat

The Rocky Mountains

The Corps of Discovery explored the Louisiana Territory and the Northwest. They were the first Americans to see this land. They saw the Great Falls of Montana. They saw the Rocky Mountains. On November 7, 1805, they saw the Pacific Ocean for the first time.

Antelope

Coyote

Grizzly bear

Lewis and Clark met about 40 Native American tribes. Many of these tribes were friendly.

Lewis and Clark saw animals they had never seen before. They saw grizzly bears, coyotes, prairie dogs, and antelope. They brought back many animals and plants.

The Corps of Discovery often faced danger. Crossing the Rocky Mountains was difficult. Many became sick. Sometimes, they ran out of food. Mosquitoes, flies, and fleas often troubled them, too.

The beautiful West was full of danger.

Sacagawea

Lewis and Clark made friends on the expedition. They met a French Canadian trader. His name was Toussaint Charbonneau. His wife was Sacagawea. Sacagawea was Native American. She was from the Shoshone tribe.

A statue of Sacagawea.

Native Americans often helped Lewis and Clark.

Toussaint and Sacagawea joined the expedition. They were very helpful, especially Sacagawea. She found roots and fruit for them to eat. She helped to guide the expedition to the Pacific Ocean. Sacagawea is honored today for helping Lewis and Clark.

Returning Home

On September 23, 1806, Lewis and Clark returned to St. Louis, Missouri. Almost everyone was surprised. They thought Lewis and Clark were lost or dead.

MISSOURI

St. Louis ★

Corps of Discovery

Everyone treated the Corps of Discovery like heroes. The village of St. Louis gave them a warm welcome. The United States gave Lewis and Clark 1,600 acres (647 ha) of land each. The other men received 320 acres (129 ha) of land each.

Lewis and Clark's

Into the Unknown West!

WASHINGTON

NORTH DAKOTA

MONTANA

OREGON

IDAHO

SOUTH DAKOTA

WYOMING

IOWA

NEBRASKA

KANSAS

MISSOURI

N

W — E

S

Westbound Route

Exciting Journey

Back Home in Triumph!

- Eastbound Route Together
- Lewis's Route East
- Clark's Route East

WASHINGTON

NORTH DAKOTA

MONTANA

OREGON

IDAHO

SOUTH DAKOTA

WYOMING

NEBRASKA

IOWA

KANSAS

MISSOURI

N

W · E

S

American Heroes

   Lewis and Clark were great explorers. They made maps of the land they explored. They wrote down everything that happened on their trip. They discovered 178 new plants and 122 new animals. These important maps and notes helped people to settle on America's western frontier.

   Both Meriwether Lewis and William Clark are heroes. Together, they made the expedition a success.

Lewis and Clark are American heroes.

Important Dates

August 1, 1770 William Clark was born.

August 18, 1774 Meriwether Lewis was born.

February 28, 1803 The United States decides to explore the Western United States.

June 20, 1803 President Jefferson asks Lewis to lead an exploration of the West.

May 14, 1804 Lewis and Clark begin their expedition.

Winter 1804-1805 The Corps of Discovery stop near villages of the Mandan and Hidatsa Indians. They stay there for the winter. There, they meet Toussaint Charbonneau and Sacagawea.

May 26, 1805 Clark sees the Rocky Mountains for the first time.

November 7, 1805 Lewis and Clark reach the Pacific Ocean.

September 23, 1806 St. Louis, Missouri welcomes back the Corps of Discovery.

October 1809 Lewis dies.

September 1, 1838 Clark dies.

Important Words

American Revolutionary War the war between Americans and the British. The Americans won their freedom from the British.

expedition a trip to find something new.

explorers people who closely look at something new.

frontier land that has not been settled by people.

Louisiana Territory a big piece of land the United States bought from France in 1803.

militia people who help the army in times of need, they are not soldiers.

Native Americans the very first people who lived in America.

Web Sites

Lewis & Clark: The Journey of the Corps of Discovery
http://www.pbs.org/lewisandclark/
This in-depth site features information on the members of the expedition, journal excerpts, insight from historians, and a game in which the player leads the expedition.

Go West across America with Lewis & Clark
http://www.nationalgeographic.com/west/main.html
Explore new territory, meet friendly Native Americans, map rivers, and find a Northwest Passage as a member of Lewis and Clark's expedition.

Index